SERIES EDITOR: MARTIN WINDROW

MEN-AT-ARMS 341

BRITISH AIR FORCES 1914-18 (1)

TEXT BY
ANDREW CORMACK

COLOUR PLATES BY
PETER CORMACK

First published in 2000 by Osprey Publishing,
Elms Court, Chapel Way, Botley, Oxford OX2 9LP, United Kingdom
E-mail: info@ospreypublishing.com

ISBN 1 84176 001 3

Editor: Martin Windrow
Design: Alan Hamp
Originated by Colourpath, London, UK
Printed in China through World Print Ltd

00 01 02 03 04   10 9 8 7 6 5 4 3 2 1

FOR A CATALOGUE OF ALL TITLES PUBLISHED BY OSPREY MILITARY,
AUTOMOTIVE AND AVIATION PLEASE WRITE TO:
The Marketing Manager, Osprey Publishing Ltd, PO Box 140,
Wellingborough, Northants NN8 4ZA, United Kingdom
Email: info@ospreydirect.co.uk

The Marketing Manager, Osprey Direct USA, PO Box 130,
Sterling Heights, MI 48311-0310, USA
Email: info@ospreydirectusa.com

VISIT OSPREY AT:
www.ospreypublishing.com

Dedication

This book is dedicated to Dr.John Tanner, CBE, FRAeS, FSA, MA, PhD
founding Director of the Royal Air Force Museum, Hendon (1965-1988)
in tribute to his vision, determination and liberal collecting policies.

Author's Note

I am very greatly indebted to the following individuals and
institutions for their assistance in the preparation of this book:
Pat Blackett-Barber, Henry Blagg, Dr.Peter Boyden, William
Carman, Sandra Coley, Rog Dennis, Keith Hook, Sue Lindsay, Bob
Marrion, Helen McCorry, Graham Muir, Joan and Tony Poucher,
William Spencer, The National Army Museum, the Fleet Air Arm
Museum, the Imperial War Museum, the Public Records Office, and
the Scottish United Services Museum. Special thanks are due to my
brother, Peter, for the colour illustrations; and to my wife, Helen, for
her patience, understanding and support.

Artist's Note

Readers may care to note that the original paintings from which the
colour plates in this book were prepared are available for private
sale. All reproduction copyright whatsoever is retained by the
Publishers. All enquiries should be addressed to:

Peter Cormack, c/o 9A Woodside Lane, London N12 8RB, UK
Email: pdc@wolfofgubbio.freeserve.co.uk

The Publishers regret that they can enter into no correspondence
upon this matter.

BRITISH AIR FORCES 1914-18 (1) UNIFORMS OF THE RFC AND RNAS

THE MILITARY AIR SERVICES

2nd Lt V.G.A. Bush wearing the later version of the 1912 Pattern RFC officers' Service Dress ('maternity') jacket, with lapel extended to the right shoulder; under magnification the vertical slit pockets can be made out below the line of the belt. Note the distinctive flare of the Officers' breeches compared to Other Ranks' pantaloons. (RAFM Box 536)

THE MILITARY USE OF BALLOONS started at the end of the 18th century, but it was only in 1878 that the British Army began to interest itself in aerial matters, after the real usefulness of hydrogen-filled observation balloons had been demonstrated in the Franco-Prussian War. Balloons accompanied Field Forces to the Sudan in 1885, and in 1890 a Balloon Section was formed within the Royal Engineers. Three Balloon Sections served in South Africa during the Boer War, but the branch was always kept on a very tight budget and the War Office showed no great enthusiasm for aeronautical soldiering. This trend continued even after the advent of powered flight, despite both the increasing technical prowess and the undisguised military interest shown by both France and Germany in the new science of aviation.

Public attention in Great Britain was seized in July 1909 when Louis Bleriot crossed the English Channel by aeroplane; and over the next few years the Press, and generous private individuals, tried to shake the War Office out of its complacency. However, it was not until 1911 that a Royal Engineers Air Battalion was formed; its one hundred and fifty men, in two companies, were to be instructed in the use of balloons, man-carrying kites and aeroplanes. Eventually continuing public pressure obliged the government to look into the development of military aviation, and the result was a recommendation to form a new service, the Royal Flying Corps, to comprise Military and Naval 'Wings' and a joint-service Central Flying School. The force came into existence on 13 April 1912.

Almost immediately, and despite the good will of the officers actually engaged in flying, the two Wings began to drift apart. The War Office and the Admiralty were unable to agree on a common policy for the development of aviation which would meet the requirements of their two forces, and by July 1914 the *de facto* split was acknowledged by the independent formation of the Royal Naval Air Service. Thereafter the RFC became the Army's air branch and was no longer the joint-service organisation which it was originally intended to be.

When the Great War commenced a few weeks later the RFC's aircraft strength was 179, and its mobilised, uniformed personnel totalled just 2,073 officers and men under the command of BrigGen Sir David Henderson. The Army took four squadrons to France equipped with a mixed bag of unarmed biplanes and monoplanes. The RNAS had 39 landplanes and 52 seaplanes dotted around the coast, and seven airships intended to provide long range reconnaissance for the Fleet. No provision was made for aeronautical support to any British overseas territories.

By 31 March 1918 the RFC had 56 squadrons serving on the Western Front; 68, including Training Squadrons, in the UK; and 18 squadrons in Italy, Africa, Palestine, Mesopotamia, the Balkans and India in addition to dozens of observation balloon units. The RNAS stood at 16 squadrons in France, and had numerous flights scattered around the UK and the Mediterranean, plus 90 airships patrolling Home Waters. Extensive support facilities and training units backed up these forces, including schools in Canada and Texas. Most of these resources were recombined on 1 April 1918 to form the world's largest, and first independent, air service – the Royal Air Force.

THE ROYAL FLYING CORPS

Service Dress – Officers

Although the new Corps was born in April 1912 the amendment which introduced the Royal Flying Corps into the Army's 1911 Dress Regulations had to wait until Army Order 378 of November 1913 (AO378/13). This was evidently a consolidation order for a set of uniform which had evolved since the spring of 1912.

All garments were khaki unless stated otherwise, and similarly Officers' badges and buttons were bronze whilst Other Ranks' examples were of gilding metal. The first cap to be worn by Officers of the Corps was the universal pattern fabric **peaked cap** of 1902, and this remained in use throughout the Corps' existence. Sergeant-majors were issued with the peaked cap of 1904 and men with the 1908 Pattern, and these were the predominant headdresses until the winter of 1913. The cap badge was composed of the letters RFC in monogram within a crowned wreath.

By autumn 1913 a different cap was introduced and was initially referred to as the 'Austrian' pattern, later to be known as the **Field Service cap**. This was a folding sidecap with a band which could be let down to form a type of balaclava helmet fastening with two small buttons under the chin; the pattern dated back to 1891, and it was in use in various unit colours in several regiments. When worn normally the buttons – sometimes gilt for Officers – appeared at the front and the cap was positioned on the right side of the head, occasionally retained by a brown leather chin strap.

The Officer's jacket – soon to become known as the **'maternity' jacket**, because it was said to resemble clothing worn by expectant mothers – was of the normal length but cut with an extended flap, falling vertically from the

Other Ranks of the Army Wing and Ratings of the Naval Wing, Central Flying School, Upavon 1913. Unusually, several of the naval personnel wear 'hot climate' white dress alongside their comrades in ceremonial 'England and temperate climates' blue dress with gold badges. Note the mixture of Sennet hats and white or white-covered caps; both bear the ROYAL FLYING CORPS cap tally. (RAFM Box 194)

swell of the collar bone, which fastened with concealed buttons down the right side of the body. It had a central rear vent, shoulder straps, and a stand-and-fall collar with a narrow white false shirt collar showing above it; the plain cuffs bore a rearward pointing tab and concealed press stud, with a further fastening to tighten the tab around the wrist. The purpose of this detail was presumably to allow the cuff to be drawn in when wearing aviators' gauntlets. Vertical buttoned pockets without flaps were cut into the waist. All buttons were of horn, not metal, and the inner ends of the shoulder straps fastened with press studs. No collar badges were sanctioned. Rank appeared on the shoulder straps in pale buff and tan embroidered 'pips' and crowns, the latter always positioned above the former, according to the following table:

Rank	Pip	Crown
Colonel	2	1
Lieutenant-Colonel	1	1
Major	–	1
Captain	3	–
Lieutenant	2	–
Second Lieutenant	1	–

Capt W.V.T. Rooper, Denbigh Yeomanry and No.1 Squadron, RFC. He wears the 1908 universal pattern Officers' jacket with regimental collar badges, leather buttons, and the RFC pilot's flying badge. (RAFM PC73/60/77)

This jacket was worn with the Sam Browne **belt**, usually with only one brace over the right shoulder. Officers already possessing belts continued to wear them, and hence Light Infantry whistles and various other standard appendages appeared on the braces. Bedford cord **breeches** of special pattern – probably because they fastened at the knee with laces rather than buttons – were worn along with puttees and brown leather ankle boots. Officers of all ranks were permitted to wear brown field boots or brown leather gaiters with their ankle boots.

The uniform underwent a number of small but significant changes in the seven years of its existence but, whereas it is possible to date fairly precisely changes to Other Ranks' clothing, plotting those made to Officers' dress is more difficult. The difference in the appearance of some garments is accounted for by variations introduced by the tailor employed to make them; Officers paid for their own uniform and had it made up privately. Photographic evidence, however, reveals subtle changes which were never noted in Regulations.

Officers very soon extended the lapel flap of the jacket so that it formed a point at the shoulder and traced an elegant line to the waist. Collar badges – small versions of the cap badge – appeared as an early deviation from the regulations. The false shirt collar was often omitted. Officers adopted different styles of pocket to overcome the difficulty of using the original type when wearing the Sam Browne. Flapped pockets seem to have been most popular, sometimes horizontal, sometimes slightly sloping to the rear, but angled slash pockets without flaps were also commonly used. During 1916 some Officers discarded the cuff tabs and had their sleeves cut either plain or with false pointed cuffs, though tabs continue to appear throughout the jacket's history – some functional and some merely decorative, being stitched down all round. Rank was indicated by gilt or bronze metal pips and crowns as well as embroidered ones. Fawn or beige breeches with fabric or suede reinforcing patches became as common as khaki ones. Fabric gaiters were sported by some Officers rather than leather ones, and plain khaki trousers, which had always been part of undress uniform, were often worn.

Officers seconded to the RFC continued to wear the Service Dress of their original unit complete with cap and collar badges. The 1902 jacket closing to the neck, or the 1908 modified 'collar and tie' pattern, frequently appear in photographs of 1912 to 1914, the only RFC distinction being the flying badge for those appropriately qualified. This practice of wearing 'original unit' dress continued throughout the Corps' existence.

CFS Upavon, January 1913. Air Mechanic W.Turner (centre top) wears the 1912 Pattern jacket, second version, while Sgt F.T. McElwee (right) wears the first version – the differences in the collars and lapels are obvious. Sergeant A. Jukes (left) and Sgt H.T. Hamilton Copeland (bottom) wear the 1912 Pattern greatcoat without shoulder straps. (RAFM X001-2627)

After the war began many Officers who joined the RFC direct adopted the 1908 Pattern tunic, worn by almost all of their infantry and cavalry colleagues in preference to, or as well as, the 'maternity' pattern. In this book this garment will be referred to as the RFC Pattern 1915 Jacket. It was a four-button, single-breasted garment with stepped lapels and shoulder straps; it had bellows pockets in the skirt and pleated, patch pockets in the breast. All pocket flaps – three-pointed on the breast and straight on the skirts – closed with a small uniform button. Bronze badges were worn on the collar, and rank appeared as embroidered pips and crowns (in the same arrangements as above) on cuff patches decorated with tan lace bearing a central line of off-white chevrons. The cuff patches were traced in a single lace for all ranks but the cuff itself was outlined with one row for second lieutenants and lieutenants, two rows for captains, three rows for majors and lieutenant-colonels and four for colonels. Buttons were gilt, embossed with a crown above 'R.F.C.'. All other Service Dress clothing remained the same.

In 1916 or 1917, again in line with the practice in other branches of the Army, rank ceased to be worn on the cuff and appeared as metal or embroidered pips and crowns on the shoulder straps. The sleeves were henceforth cut with a false pointed cuff or plain. No official announcement heralded the appearance of this jacket, which may be designated the Pattern 1917. Many Officers wore 'original unit' jackets but with the RFC badge on their caps. Some sported RFC FS caps with regimental uniform. General Officers wore their special uniform with no RFC distinctions other than the flying badge if appropriate.

RFC Service Dress – Other Ranks

Many of the original RFC airmen transferred from the Air Battalion or other units and continued to wear their 1908 General Service Pattern clothing until issued with the new uniform. Their 1912 Pattern **'maternity' jacket** was cut in a style similar to that of the Officer's garment with the perpendicular lapel. It had a short central rear vent, and no shoulder straps. The fall part of the stand-and-fall collar was cut so as to show an opening. The jacket was produced in hard, hairy serge and was worn without a false shirt collar. All buttons were made of horn. From the beginning it appeared with distinctive embroidered shoulder titles, off-white on very dark blue patches, 'ROYAL FLYING' in an arc above 'CORPS' in a straight line, worn at the very top of the sleeve by all ranks without exception.

Pantaloons, cut loose in the thigh but close around the knee, were made of a fabric similar to whipcord but not as smooth, and fastened with laces at the knee. They were worn with drab puttees wound from the bottom in infantry style, and black ankle boots. After the issue of the Corps uniform GS pattern kit was retained for working dress and, in the early days at least, was worn with the full shoulder title, though during the war these were often omitted. For walking out Other Ranks carried a swagger stick made of bamboo with a white metal top.

The ORs' 'maternity' jacket underwent a series of changes before the start of the war which substantially altered its appearance. In late 1912 an Improved Pattern was introduced which extended the lapel over to the right shoulder and reduced the gap in the fall part of the collar, allowing it to be closed with a hook and eye. February 1913 saw another change to Pattern No.7763, but this appears to have been only an adjustment in the sizes in which the jacket was made. A similar resizing resulted in the issue of Pattern No.8018 in March 1914. The definitive pattern was arrived at in June 1914, when the ORs' version acquired shoulder straps, and the vertical slit pockets were replaced with horizontal pockets

The second version of the 1912 Pattern ORs' jacket; the collar is now closed and the lapel extends to the shoulder. His left hand rests just behind the vertical, buttoned slit pocket. Compare the outline of the ORs' pantaloons with the Officers' breeches on page 3. (RAFM Box 194)

at hip level closing with a buttoned flap. This gave access to the pockets even when the broad webbing belt from the 1908 Pattern Equipment set was worn. By this time the sleeves had also lost their pointed cuff-tightening tab.

The rank structure of the personnel of the RFC evolved gradually and did not reach its final form until late 1916. **Rank badges** on Service Dress garments appeared on both sleeves. Originally there were two NCO ranks only: sergeant-majors and sergeants, the former wearing a large crown on the wrist and the latter three chevrons on the upper arm (AO131/12). Corporals and flight sergeants were added in May 1914 (AO174/14), and wore respectively two chevrons, and three chevrons surmounted by a medium-sized crown above a star-boss four-bladed propeller. Sergeants added plain four-bladed propellers above their stripes. Technical quarter-master sergeants were introduced in March 1915 (AO131/15), identified by

(Left to right) Cpl McGair with Air Mechanics Page and Wakeley and one other, 4 Reserve Aeroplane Squadron, Northolt, 1915. They wear the 1914 Pattern jacket with shoulder straps and 1908 Pattern pistol equipment, though Wakeley uses the left rifle ammunition carrier.

four chevrons, points upwards, on their cuffs surmounted by a star-boss propeller. Warrant Officers Class II were authorised in January 1915 (AO70/15) and their badge introduced in May (AO174/15); they adopted the medium-sized crown formerly used by flight sergeants and wore it on the cuff – it ceased to be used thereafter by flight sergeants. At the same time Warrant Officers Class I, still usually known as sergeant-majors, were given embroidered Royal Arms cuff badges. Finally, as a consequence of the introduction of 3rd class air mechanics in October 1916, 1st class air mechanics received a horizontal two-bladed propeller appointment badge to be worn on the right upper arm only (AO311 & 322/16).

Rank chevrons were of the universal Army pattern of off-white and tan woven lace on a khaki fabric background. All rank chevrons, except those of technical quartermasters, were worn inverted – point downwards. Crowns and propeller badges were embroidered in the same colours, sometimes with black detailing. Evidence derived from the dates of the sealed patterns of these various badges indicates that sergeants' propellers may have been issued from late 1913; and that flight sergeants' crowns were not approved until June 1914, and their star-boss propellers not until 1 October. Up until this date flight sergeants appear to have used the ordinary propeller plus crown. Good Conduct chevrons, with points upwards, were worn on the left cuff in the same lace as used for rank badges. They do not seem to have been awarded after the war began.

From very early on some sergeant-majors followed their Officers and took to wearing cap badges on the collars of their jackets which, at this period, were of the same quality cloth as all Other Ranks. After mid-1915 some WOIs provided themselves with well-tailored uniforms in a much finer cloth similar to that used by Officers. They did not have shoulder titles. WOIs wore this uniform with a Sam Browne belt with right brace, and in Parade Order all WOs wore brown boots and gloves and carried a black walking stick with silver top. Some continued, unofficially, to wear collar badges. By the later war period it is also quite common to see photographs of WOs I and II wearing gilding metal rank badges.

RFC Greatcoats
Officers' greatcoats were of a special RFC pattern in thick khaki cloth cut in a similar manner to the jacket, with a fly-fastening lapel which extended only part-way to the right shoulder. Flapped horizontal pockets appeared at hip level, worsted rank badges on the shoulder straps; the sleeves had cuff tabs and there was a central rear vent. Most Officers would have brought with them their regimental or corps greatcoats, and it is clear that after the start of the war the standard 'British Warm' type of double-breasted overcoat became the most widely used form. Produced in fleece cloth of various shades of khaki or palish brown with a half-belt at the rear, central vent and shoulder straps, this was shorter and more convenient than a greatcoat. Buttons were of leather and included two or three small ones vertically on the rear of the cuff. Rank appeared in metal or embroidered badges on the shoulder straps. There were horizontal flapped pockets at hip level; British Warms were commonly cut with an open pocket in the left breast, and often fitted with a fur collar. Private purchase waterproof coats were permitted to be worn with metal rank badges on the shoulders.

The Pattern 1913 Other Ranks' greatcoat was of serge and reached to the knee. It was similar in cut to the Officer's version, but had a wide falling collar and no shoulder straps. It could be fastened to the neck by horn buttons concealed within a fly, but was often worn with the upper part turned back into false lapels. Shoulder titles appeared on the upper sleeves. As with the jackets, shoulder straps were added in June 1914.

On both jackets and greatcoats an embroidered **'R.F.C.' title** sometimes replaced the full wording. This abbreviated badge seems to originate in August 1915 when two sealed patterns, Nos.8457 and 8499, were approved within 14 days of each other. No.8499 was the full title produced in machine embroidery; No.8457 must have been the type with initials only. From 1917 onwards photographs seem to indicate that

An impeccably turned out sergeant-major, probably of 56 Training Squadron in 1917. The smooth, high quality fabric of his well-cut jacket is clearly discernible. He wears the embroidered Royal Arms badge above a wrist tab. (RAFM B977)

some RFC entrants received **General Service clothing** rather than the Corps uniform. The RFC cap badge was worn with this kit either on the FS cap or the 1915 Pattern ('Gor' Blimey') soft peaked cap, but one does not always see shoulder titles.

RFC Tropical Uniform – Officers

Very soon after the outbreak of war units of the Royal Flying Corps were posted to the Middle East or formed from cadres in Egypt, Mesopotamia (Iraq) and East Africa. Light-weight cotton Khaki Drill clothing (KD) was adopted for service in these countries; Officers seconded from other British or Indian Army units wore the style favoured by their original regiment or corps, and direct entries to the RFC acquired suits of a more or less standard cut. The clothing was produced with detachable buttons and badges so as to be easily washable, and the colour was a pale sand hue, though it varied considerably in shade due to original variations in the colour of the cloth and to fading through laundering and sun bleaching.

The jacket was single-breasted with bellows pockets in the skirt and pleated breast pockets. All closed with buttoned flaps which were normally cut straight in the skirt but could be three-pointed in the breast. Sleeves were either plain or had false pointed cuffs. Soft shoulder straps carried rank insignia in gilt or bronze pips or crowns. There was a central rear vent. Buttons appear usually to have been gilt, but bronze or leather ones were not unknown. Four main front buttons seems to have been usual, but regimental variants were common. Bronze RFC badges sometimes appear on the collar. Shirts and ties were in a multitude of pale to medium khaki hues. Breeches and trousers were made from the same fabric, the former sometimes having rubbing patches on the inside of the leg, usually of the same material, sometimes of contrasting stuff, possibly suede (though this would have made them difficult to wash). Shorts were also worn with this jacket. Headgear consisted of either of the khaki Home Service caps, a Field Service cap made up in Khaki Drill material, a pith hat or the Wolseley helmet. The latter two headdresses had narrow brown leather chin straps, and there is some evidence that a puggaree flash in the

LtCol George Dawes, CO of No.16 Wing, Salonika (centre), having just been promoted an *Officier de la Légion d'Honneur*. He wears the 1912 Pattern 'maternity' jacket while his Staff Officers wear khaki drill – note the RFC staff collar tabs on the officer to Dawes' left (cf Plate E1). (RAFM PC1996/296)

Corps colours was worn vertically on the left side. Sam Brownes complemented this kit, and the normal range of brown footwear was seen. The maternity jacket was not produced in Khaki Drill.

RFC Tropical Uniform – Other Ranks

Other Ranks present just as wide a range of variation as Officers in the tropical dress which they wore, despite the fact that their clothing was issued. The 1914 Clothing Regulations for the Army give no scale of issue of tropical kit for the RFC, but it was doubtless scarcely different from that for Royal Engineers.

The standard khaki FS cap was supplemented by a **KD Field Service cap**, a pith hat and the Wolseley helmet. At least two patterns of **KD frocks** were used, both being five-button, single-breasted garments with a stand collar, shoulder straps and two short rear vents in line with the shoulders. One version had flap-and-button breast pockets only, sometimes pleated, sometimes plain patch pockets, and the other had buttoned-flap skirt pockets as well. Buttons were gilding metal GS pattern, RFC or compressed leather type. Rank insignia and shoulder titles were worn as on the maternity jacket, though one also occasionally notices a curved gilding metal initial title worn on the shoulder straps instead of the embroidered type.

KD shorts extending to the top of the knee were issued with this jacket; and also short KD trousers which reached to the upper calf. These were designed to be turned up by about 6 inches (15cm) and fastened with a small button on the outer seam to convert them to shorts during daylight hours, but could be let down and bound in with the puttees in the evening as a protection against mosquitos. There is also evidence of KD pantaloons being worn as well as trousers. Puttees were the same greenish khaki as for Home Service and footwear was the standard black ankle boot.

The tropics were the place for 'scruff order' par excellence, and the collarless pale grey flannel shirt with rolled sleeves was the usual working dress.

A sergeant in the four-pocket Army KD jacket, the buttons of which appear to be leather. He wears the Home Service khaki Field Service cap, and puttees. (RAFM PC1998/49/3)

RFC Full Dress – All Ranks

Army Order 378 described the Full Dress for the RFC in its final form, but some debate had evidently taken place as to the style and the colour of this form of dress. The undated Sealed Pattern No. 7679 of August or September 1912 deals with a light blue cloth which must have been

LEFT **Sgt Alfred Cook, 17th Lancers transferred RFC, immaculately turned out and still sporting his marksman and skill-at-arms (crossed lances) badges on the forearm as well as his RFC observer's badge on the left breast.**

RFC Other Ranks' Full Dress, Aldershot, 1913. The film emulsion does not pick up the difference between scarlet and dark blue, but the arrangement of the gilt collar and shoulder strap badges and gold lace Good Conduct stripes leaves no doubt what this uniform is. (RAFM Box 26)

intended for Full Dress and which was made up into a trial jacket, now in the collection of the Imperial War Museum. It was similar in cut to that worn by Lancer regiments, having a dark blue plastron front, collar and pointed cuffs, the latter two elements trimmed with blue Russia braid, which also appeared on the rear skirts. The plastron was fastened by two gilt buttons on each shoulder, but the right side closed with concealed buttons.

Though the reasons for its rejection are unknown, this pattern was replaced by a less cavalry-style dress in very dark blue faced with scarlet. The cut was essentially the same for all ranks. The cap was of the universal peaked type with a gilt badge for Officers, gilding metal for Other Ranks, scarlet band and welt around the crown and a black leather peak and chin strap, the latter retained by tiny RFC buttons. Field Officers would have had their peaks decorated with one-inch flat gold embroidery. The jacket was single-breasted with scarlet collar and pointed cuffs, and closed with eight buttons for Officers, seven for Other Ranks. The front opening was piped in scarlet down its full length. All collars were given the appearance of being piped in scarlet. On the Officer's jacket the front and top edges of the collar bore a slightly inset ⅝in (16mm) dark blue mohair lace; a narrow Russia braid of the same stuff encircled the base of the collar. The wide braid was also used to outline the cuffs, but was applied so as to cover the join between the sleeve and the facing leaving no scarlet showing above. The point of the cuff lace was padded so as to give it prominence but the rest of the lace was applied flat.

Both the collars and cuffs of sergeant-majors and quartermaster sergeants were trimmed with ⁹⁄₁₆in (14mm) lace set in so as to show a piping, as were those of flight sergeants and sergeants, which used ³⁄₁₆in (5mm) braid; no Russia braid appeared at the base of their collars, however. Air mechanics of both classes had plain collars and cuffs. Collars carried gilt or gilding metal badges. Two buttons appeared at the rear waist and the box-pleated false vent in the skirts was figured with three pairs of loops of Russia braid. Officers' jackets were provided with twisted round-section gold shoulder cords, lined with blue cloth, bearing embroidered rank badges, whilst all ORs had plain shoulder straps. These carried slightly curved gilding metal titles of the Corps' initials, with each letter voided and linked to its neighbours at top and bottom only.

All ranks wore a 2½in-wide blue Petersham girdle, silk for both Officers and Other Ranks, which fastened at the left side with three small olivets – gold wire for Officers, gilding metal for Other Ranks. Trousers were close fitting for Officers, cut round the boot and strapped under the instep; they were less snug for ORs. All carried a 2-in scarlet side stripe. Boots were of Wellington pattern for officers, laced ankle pattern without toe caps for ORs. No mention is made in AO378/13 of Officers wearing swords in Full Dress, and as no photographs exist of it being worn it is impossible to say whether they did so or not. As Officers of even non-combatant corps, such as the Veterinary Corps and the Postal Corps, did wear swords, it would have been exceptional for the RFC not to have done so; evidence, however, is entirely lacking. Officers, in conformity with all their colleagues, would have worn white gloves.

NCOs wore badges of rank which had been approved up to the date of the introduction of Full Dress in the same forms as on Service Dress, but in gold lace and/or gold embroidery, and on the right sleeve only. Men entitled to Long Service stripes wore them as chevrons above the left cuff in gold lace.

The patterns for the ORs' Full Dress garments were sealed between October and December 1913 and examples exist in the RAF Museum collection. It was certainly issued to the original members of the Corps, and photographs exist to prove it, though it can have been worn on very few occasions. It was laid aside following AO292 of 1 September 1914 which restricted all units except the Guards and the Household Cavalry to Service Dress for the duration of the war. Only Officers entering the Corps by way of the Special Reserve – i.e. as direct entrants, not seconded – would have required this kit, and in consequence very few sets can have been made.

Mess Dress

In accordance with normal peacetime expectations Mess Dress was included in AO378. The colours adopted were dark blue and scarlet, and it was cut along infantry lines rather than in cavalry style. The single-breasted, waist-length jacket closed with four gilt buttons and had a wide roll collar and cuffs in scarlet, the buttoned shoulder straps being dark blue. Rank insignia in gilt metal crowns and pips appeared on the latter, whilst the collar bore gilt Corps badges in the usual form on the chest. The points of the cuffs were 6ins deep tapering to 2¾ins behind. The dark blue waistcoat was cut very low, revealing a stiff white shirtfront worn with gold studs, wing collar and black bow tie. All buttons were flat, with the crown and RFC finely engraved upon them and filled in black. Full Dress trousers were worn with Wellington boots. Field Officers – majors and above – wore them with burnished steel box spurs plugged into the heels. Attached Officers continued to wear the mess dress of their original units.

RFC Patrol Dress

Despite the discontinuance of Mess and Full Dress from September 1914, Patrol Dress remained an optional extra form of uniform for Officers. It was used for walking-out purposes and when the Officer was not on duty. Four versions of the jacket exist in the RAF Museum collection, and

Lt W.K. Rose and 2nd Lt J.F. Ridgway of No.7 Squadron clearly displaying the differences at cuffs and shoulder straps between the Army Officers' 1917 Pattern Service Dress jacket (left) and the 1915 Pattern (right). (RAFM AC1998/61/28)

they all differ one from another. In three of the garments the differences are of detail only, but in one there is a major divergence of style. The jacket was produced in a rich dark blue fabric with gilt buttons and gilt rank badges on the shoulder straps, and was worn with the Full Dress cap, trousers and boots and, usually, the Sam Browne belt with right brace.

The three similar versions present a single-breasted, five-button, four-pocket jacket, with shoulder straps and false pointed cuffs. All have stand collars with a false white shirt collar fastened inside leaving a narrow strip just visible above. Breast pockets are cut either with a pleat or as plain patch pockets and all have three-point flaps with buttons. Captain Reginald Stocken's jacket of July 1917 has small RFC buttons throughout, straight flap-and-button lower pocket flaps set on false gusseted pockets, a central rear vent and a removable fabric belt with a single-prong gilt frame buckle, though it also has brass hooks at either side of the waist to support a Sam Browne. Lieutenant Pellew's jacket of September 1917 bears collar badges and has large buttons for the opening and small ones on the straight pocket flaps set over gusseted pockets. It has a central vent and is cut for wear with a Sam Browne. A third version made by Burberry's has two shallow rear vents in line with the shoulders, large and small buttons, and was not intended to be worn with a belt. Both breast and skirt pockets have three-pointed flaps with buttons on plain patch pockets.

Late in the war a different type was unofficially introduced, cut in exactly the same style as the 1917 Pattern Officers' Service Dress jacket. The example in the Museum's collection was made for Major William Barker VC, the fighter ace. It was worn with a white shirt with normal stiff, fold-down collar and a long black tie.

RFC Working Clothing

Apart from the use of GS pattern garments as working dress the mechanics of the RFC required other more suitable clothing in which to undertake their airframe and engine-fitting duties. The first set of overalls was the Pattern 1912 and was known as the Suit, Combination, Jean, Blue. It was an all-in-one garment with a shallow stand collar, an adjustable half-belt across the back, side pockets and a patch pocket on the left breast. It closed with buttons concealed in a fly and appears to have had a buttoned cuff. 'Jean' referred to the type of fabric from which it was made and the colour was a darkish Royal blue. It was not worn with badges of rank.

Alongside this another older, probably two-piece fatigue suit was in use, designated Pattern 6102B of 1898 . Both this and the blue combination suit were superseded by the 1915 Pattern garment, which was made in brown cotton drill material. In September 1916 another pattern was introduced, this time in white kersey fabric; and the available range was further supplemented in January 1917 by Overalls, Drab, made up from the same fabric as was used for greatcoats – surely a most cumbersome and restrictive garment to wear, though presumably necessary as a winter alternative. It was followed two months later by another khaki overall, but this time produced in cotton drill. The shape of all of these suits appears to be the

ABOVE **Maj S.H. Long, DSO, MC, wearing the second version of Officers' Patrol Dress with collar and tie. Unlike Maj Barker, VC, he wears no collar badges on this uniform, but does sport the same gold wire wings. As a Field Officer he should have a plain, broad gold lace to his cap peak, but this is missing. (RAFM Box 552)**

The comfortable and convenient British Warm with leather buttons, breast pocket and optional fur collar. (RAFMPC73/78/11)

same. As will be readily appreciated the blue, brown and khaki cotton variants are very difficult to tell apart in monochrome photographs.

RFC Webbing Equipment

Though the absence of shoulder straps from the first Other Ranks' jackets implies that it was not anticipated that the RFC would wear webbing equipment, by 1914 the matter had obviously been reconsidered. The Corps was one of those which was armed with revolvers and, when armed at all, it is normally with this weapon that one sees all ranks equipped. Rifles were obviously available for guard duty in particular, but it is very rare indeed to find photographs of RFC personnel in the full 1908 Pattern webbing equipment. When rifles were used, the men almost always wore a reduced set of equipment comprising belt, braces, brace attachments and bayonet frog, and only occasionally do photographs indicate the use of ammunition carriers. Reference should be made to Men-at-Arms 108, *British Infantry Equipments 1908-1980 (Revised)*, for details of the set.

Royal Flying Corps Badges

More than any other service the RFC has become known by its most novel and distinctive badge which, in popular perception, has come to represent all its members, whether they were flyers or not. The Pilot's Flying Badge, consisting of a double-winged, crowned wreath enclosing the 'RFC' monogram, was approved by Army Order 40 of 1913 for use by Officers and Airmen whilst they remained efficient as pilots. It was followed in September 1915 by a badge for Observer Officers comprising a single-winged 'O' (AO327), and the use of this badge was extended to all ranks of qualified observers in October by AO404. Both badges for Service Dress were produced in off-white worsted embroidery on black patches, with a bright mid-brown wreath for pilots.

Numerous tailors' variants of these badges are known with different numbers of feathers in the wings and, for the pilot's badge, wreaths of various colours. Some crowns also have red inserts within the arches. For wear with Full Dress a very handsome version of the pilot's badge was produced in silver gilt and was used by all qualified ranks. A miniature silver gilt version was made for Mess Dress. The Full Dress pilot's badge was also to be worn on Patrol Dress, but was replaced during the war with one embroidered in metal wire, the wings, wreath and crown being in gold, the latter having red within the arches and the monogram 'RFC' in silver, all on a black patch.

Signallers within the RFC were distinguished in both Service and Full Dress by a crossed flags badge in drab silk or gold wire, the left flag plain blue, the right flag white with a blue horizontal central stripe. As the Corps very quickly came to depend on wireless telegraphy this badge is

OPPOSITE **2nd Lt L.G. Costa in FS cap and 1914 Pattern 'maternity' jacket, carrying his fur-lined 'British Warm' coat, in winter 1917. (RAFM Costa Papers)**

Airman of the Hampshire Aircraft Parks Battalion, Territorial Force. This is the only known view of a member of this unit with the gilding metal badge on the shoulder strap of the 1915 War Economy GS pattern jacket. (Courtesy R.J. Marrion Collection)

very rare, but photographs of it in use do exist, showing it worn on the right upper arm above the rank stripes. No other trades or skills were acknowledged by badges in the Corps.

A gilding metal shoulder strap badge made up of 'T' over 'RFC' over 'HANTS', the latter arranged in an arc, was introduced for the Hampshire Aircraft Parks, Territorial Force. This battalion was raised in November 1915 from the staff of the Royal Aircraft Factory, Farnborough, and was intended to provide repair units in the event of the war becoming mobile on the Western Front. The battalion was never embodied for service but remained in existence until 1919.

The expansion of the Corps during 1915 gave rise to an increase in **Staff Officers**, who were distinguished by an armband in July that year. The first version was French grey (a pale grey-blue) with Royal blue edges and a central red stripe; but this was obviously not sufficiently recognisable, as a second version with large Royal blue letters 'RFC' overlaying the centre stripe was produced in February 1916. These large distinctions were replaced by gorget patches of French grey bearing a central crimson gimp in August 1917 (AO237).

The latter were worn on both the lapelled 1915 and 1917 jackets and also on the collars of the 'maternity' jacket, though in both cases it was impossible to wear the bronze collar badges with them. A French grey cap band was supposed to be worn with these decorations but it does not seem to have been used. Cap bands of broad white tape were also used to distinguish Officer Cadets and were worn on peaked caps and overlaying the folded band of the FS cap.

Air mechanics wearing the 1914 Pattern greatcoat with shoulder straps. Note the line of the opening, falling straight from the collar. (RAFM B977)

THE ROYAL NAVAL AIR SERVICE

Home Service Dress – Officers

When the Naval Wing of the Royal Flying Corps was set up in April 1912 no special uniform was provided for its personnel. The RNAS, as it quickly but unofficially came to be called, constituted part of the Military Branch of the service as distinct from the Civil Branch which comprised those Officers specialising in engineering, accounting/pay, secretarial or medical work exclusively. The modifications to standard naval dress associated with the new Air Service were not codified until July 1914, by which time the Naval Wing of the RFC had formally broken away and had been officially constituted as the Royal Naval Air Service. For the first 16 months of its existence, therefore, no particular distinction marked an Officer's transfer into the new service. Officers already belonging to the Military Branch were ordered to wear standard naval uniform, all garments being of ultra dark blue.

Working Dress, which equated to the Army's Service Dress, consisted of a **peaked cap** with black mohair band and patent leather peak and chin strap, the latter retained by black, fabric covered buttons. The badge was made up of two sprays of laurel leaves enclosing a silver metal fouled anchor, the whole surmounted by a crown. The latter was embroidered in gold and full colours, the arches being filled with crimson velvet; the sprays were in gold wire. In addition the two senior RNAS Officer ranks had a row of gold oakleaf embroidery on their blue fabric-covered peaks. During the summer, 1 May to 30 September, the crown of the cap was encased in a white cover.

The so-called **'monkey' jacket** was double-breasted with a roll-step collar, eight gilt RN buttons showing a crowned fouled anchor within a rope border, no shoulder straps and two shallow rear vents. In line with the top left side button was a slightly angled breast pocket without a flap. Two horizontal slit pockets appeared in line with the hips. Rank was worn in gold lace on the cuff according to the table below, Officers of the Military Branch being entitled to wear the 'executive curl', the loop of lace emerging centrally from the topmost ring. The jacket was worn with a single-breasted, six-button **waistcoat** cut so as not to show at the collar opening of the jacket, a white shirt with a wing collar and a long black tie. **Trousers** or breeches and puttees were worn with black shoes or boots. In Parade Order brown leather gloves were worn.

With respect to the basic garments, the uniform remained the same throughout the war for Officers serving within the United Kingdom. In June 1916 (AdWO 1290) grey trousers were permitted for working duties on airfields or in hot weather, and soft turned-down shirt collars were also allowed. Soft grey shirts were permitted for

A motor transport driver well wrapped up in a heavily lined, fur collared overall coat fastened with large hooks – probably an Army Service Corps garment rather than a strictly RFC one. (RAFM PC 73/77/83)

Commander J.C. Porte, the great exponent and designer of flying boats, wears the standard 'monkey' jacket with the RNAS eagle above the 'executive curl' of his cuff ranking; his cap badge and buttons bear the RN fouled anchor. (RAFM AC78/13)

working dress during 1917. RNAS Officers on land service duties which required them to march wore ankle boots with mid-calf black leather gaiters which fastened at the sides with interconnected cord loops and a strap around the top.

Rank was indicated by a series of rings of straight-sided medium or narrow width lace encircling the jacket cuff. Broad lace was reserved for commodores and senior ranks, which rarely applied in the RNAS.

Rank	Medium	Narrow
Wing Captain	4	–
Wing Commander	3	–
Squadron Commander	2	1
Flight Commander	2	–
Flight Lieutenant	2	–
Flight Sub-Lieutenant	1	–
Probationary Flight Officer	–	–

Squadron commanders' narrow lace was positioned between the other two. Probationary flight officers, introduced in August 1916 (AdWO 2027) wore midshipmens' uniform but without white collar patches and with the eagle alone above the cuff.

RNAS Service and Flying Badges

In July 1914 Officers already belonging to the Military Branch were ordered to wear a gilt metal eagle above the executive curl on the left cuff only. Those who transferred in from the Civil Branch adopted the Military Branch lace of their RN rank and the eagle. Direct entrants to the Air Service were ordered to wear the appropriate Military Branch uniform with lace indicating their RNAS rank with the eagle, and to have a special cap badge and buttons bearing an eagle flying to the wearer's left instead of the fouled anchor. It was also anticipated that the eagle would appear on Full Dress epaulette straps and on the sword belt clasps. As part of the RN's Military Branch the eagle on the cap badge was of silver.

Officers of the Civil Branch wore gold anchors and continued to do so even if attached to perform their Civil Branch duties at an RNAS station, e.g. as Medical Officers. In practice the number of Officers who transferred into the RNAS before the start of the war was very small indeed, and apart from this original group all new entrants wore RNAS cap badges and buttons as opposed to RN ones. For the majority therefore the gilt buttons bore a crown and eagle within a roped border.

It seems to be the case that the Admiralty anticipated that all Officers serving in the RNAS would undertake flying duties and that the latter were synonymous with piloting aeroplanes. The addition of the eagle to ordinary Military Branch dress was therefore all that was required to differentiate these Officers both as regards their attachment to the new service and their function within it. Whereas this may have been true in the very early days, once the war started it ceased to be so, though it took a while for clarification – of a sort – to emerge. Admiralty Weekly Order 756 of April 1916 mentioned that Officers graded as Flying Officers, i.e. all those on flying duties, should wear an additional smaller gilt eagle on their left shoulder straps. This was clear enough in principle – but it ignored the fact that their Home Service uniform jacket did not have shoulder straps. The order was, however, applied to greatcoats and other forms of clothing which did possess them. It also specifically extended the use of the eagle on left cuff and shoulder strap to those Officers not graded as Flying Officers, but who were under a continuous obligation to make ascents in aircraft – either aeroplanes or airships – that is to say, to observers. Officers of the RNAS whose duties did not include flying at all were obliged to remove any eagles they may have been wearing, and they were therefore only distinguishable by their cap badge and buttons. In retrospect therefore it seems clear that the original expression '... graded as Flying Officers...' was intended to mean pilots, and that the cuff eagle was to denote this particular skill, though the orders of 1 July 1914 did not make this clear.

By mid-spring 1916, therefore, both pilots and observers were wearing eagles and were indistinguishable from each other. This position persisted for 14 months and was then overtaken by two changes in quick succession. On 8 June 1917, by AdWO 2106, Flying Officers were ordered to wear eagles on both cuffs and shoulder straps. This was quickly followed by AdWO 2322 of 22 June, in which observers were ordered to replace their cuff and shoulder strap eagles with a gilt badge made up of an 'O' with wings on either side. It was also envisaged that this device would appear on their buttons, Full Dress epaulettes and sword belt clasps. Although the badge was certainly produced and worn on the cuffs, and a smaller version on straps, it appears never to have been applied to buttons and was never added to the other elements of Full Dress clothing (which, in any case, had been discontinued for the rest of the war as from 1 January 1916). Probationary observer officers wore cuff badges without rank lace.

* * *

Weekly Order 2106 also introduced modifications to pilot Officers' rank insignia to make clear the increased responsibilities of those holding **appointments** above their ranks. Wing captains of commander rank used commander's lace (three rings) with a six-pointed, gold wire embroidered star above. Squadron commanders with less than eight years' seniority wore flight lieutenant's lace (two rings) with two stars vertically above the cuff eagles. Flight commanders holding the rank of flight lieutenant used lieutenant's lace (two rings) with one gold star above the eagles to indicate their command. Exactly the same additions to rank lace were applied to observer Officers holding appointments above their ranks (AdWO 4590 December 1917), the stars appearing above the winged 'O' badge. When two stars were worn on greatcoat straps they appeared side by side and in half the size of the cuff stars.

The rank of **Warrant Officer** in the Royal Navy was conferred upon the most highly skilled and long-serving tradesmen in their speciality. They constituted the lowest strata of the RN Officer branch – as opposed to their Army namesakes, who constituted the highest level of the NCO branch. Naval Warrant Officers were divided into two grades and all used Officer's pattern clothing; those serving in the RNAS wore the special cuff eagles, cap badge and buttons of that branch. Within the two grades, trade rating, seniority and rank overlaid each other producing a structure of great complexity. All WOs wore three buttons horizontally on the cuff, and in addition Chief WOs wore, above, a single ½ in gold

Flight Sub-Lieutenant W.F. Davenport, late summer 1917; note the eagles now worn on both cuffs, and the white cap cover. (RAFM Box 144)

lace with executive curl; WOs of ten years' seniority wore a single ⅛in lace, and WOs of less seniority wore the buttons only.

RNVR and RNR

Once the war started many Officers were recalled from the Reserve Forces and it is not uncommon to see their distinctive lace in photographs. The **Royal Naval Volunteer Reserve** (RNVR) used ⅜in lace applied in an undulating line, and was consequently known as the 'Wavy Navy'. The intermediate lace of lieutenant-commanders RNVR was, however, straight. The **Royal Naval Reserve** (RNR) used two ⅜in laces arranged to cross over each other, thereby forming a series of oval horizontal loops in a chain pattern round the cuff. Officers of the Military Branches of both Reserves were entitled to the executive curl, which was either wavy or set in a rather angular looped style as appropriate; however, no provision was made to enable them to indicate that they were serving with the RNAS. As a consequence many of them adopted, unofficially, the cuff eagle whether or not they were engaged on flying duties.

This was disallowed for those not so engaged by AdWO 756 of 21 April 1916, and only those who were graded as Flying Officers or under a continuous liability to fly were permitted to continue to wear the eagle on the left cuff and shoulder strap. The position was further defined by AdWO 1865 of August 1916 which specifically restricted the use of the eagle to 'Acceptance Officers' holding pilot's certificates and to observers. This remained the position until November of the following year (AdWO 4284), when a new gilt badge was introduced consisting of an 'A' (for Air) with wings, which was to be worn by RNR and RNVR Officers attached to the RNAS in place of the eagle badges on both cuffs and shoulder straps. Reserve Officers graded as Flying Officers retained the eagle and the Air Branch badge was restricted to those engaged in ground duties only.

RNAS Officers' Greatcoats

RNAS Officers wore the long RN double-breasted greatcoat which fell to 14 inches from the ground. It had six pairs of buttons set 4ins apart at the waist and gradually widening to 5¼ins apart at the shoulder. Shoulder boards showed rank lace with curl exactly as on the jacket cuffs, plus, in due course, eagle and star badges as described above. The coat had a half-belt at the rear with gilt buttons at either end, a full length back pleat and a vent which fastened with four small plain buttons. There were no pockets or cuffs, but a horizontal slit for the sword to emerge when worn with Full Dress appeared at the waist. A shorter, knee-length garment, double-breasted with five buttons on each side, flapped pockets, soft shoulder straps, a centre vent but no rear belt was also introduced by AdWO 991 of May 1916 under the title of a Watch Coat. A third overcoat-type garment was used as flying clothing and will be dealt with in the second volume covering that kit. Black waterproof gabardine coats and, for working wear, oilskins were also allowed.

RNAS Service Dress – Ratings

Naval uniform for non-commissioned ranks in 1912 was divided into three classes. Class I applied to Chief Petty Officers, the equivalents of Army sergeant-majors; Class II was provided for petty officers and men 'dressed as seamen', while Class III was for non-seamen Ratings. Apart from the senior NCO grade, therefore, a very clear division was made between those who 'worked the ship' and those who provided support services afloat or in shore establishments.

When the Naval Wing of the Royal Flying Corps was formed applications to transfer were invited from Ratings whose skills might be useful to the fledgling service, and it was inevitable that most of those who transferred would come from the Class II group rather than those employed in administrative, catering,

Detail from a group photograph of Chief Petty Officers of RNAS Chingford, autumn 1915. Almost all wear gilt metal collar eagles, including the man in khaki Overseas Service Dress. Seated flanking the Officer, note Chief Yeoman of Signals (left) and Gun Layer 1st Class (right). (RAFM DB33)

medical or clerical work. Thus it is that the very first photographs of the Naval Wing feature wood-working artificers and engineering tradesmen wearing the seamen's dress of the period.

Class II seamen's clothing was provided in two sets: in dark blue serge for wear in the United Kingdom and temperate climates, and in white cotton for wear in hot climates. With blue clothing the inner body garment was a white vest, its square-cut neck bound in blue tape. Over this was worn a very short 'waistcoat' fastening with tapes, the sole purpose of which was to carry the mid-blue jean collar edged in three rows of narrow white tape. Over this combination was worn a dark blue V-neck serge jumper with cuffs fastened by two black horn buttons. The laced collar was arranged over this outer garment, and a black silk kerchief was worn under the collar, secured by tapes at the base of the V-neck opening, and decorated with the white clasp knife lanyard arranged around it. The knife fitted into an internal pocket in the left breast. Dark blue 'bell bottomed' trousers completed the outfit, which was worn with blue socks and black half boots.

White clothing consisted of a cotton duck outer jumper with the laced blue jean collar permanently attached. The bottom of this garment and the ends of the sleeves were bound in blue tape. The inner white vest bound in blue at the neck was the same as with the blue uniform, as were the kerchief and lanyard. Trousers were white and black shoes were permitted with this set.

Headgear consisted of a dark blue cap in winter, and in summer either a white duck cap or a broad-brimmed Sennet hat made of straw and bound in black tape. This could be worn with either uniform as a protection against the sun. All headdresses could be secured by inch-wide blue worsted chin tapes sewn as a loop to the inner band and normally tucked inside the crown. Around the cap and the Sennet hat a traditional black silk cap tally appeared bearing ROYAL FLYING CORPS in gold letters; this fastened with a decorative bow on the left side. After July 1914 a version bearing ROYAL NAVAL AIR SERVICE was produced.

It must quickly have become evident that this clothing was a very inappropriate dress for air service duties and by July 1914 direct entrants to the RNAS received Class III kit. It is uncertain whether all of those who had transferred from ships' duties were rekitted as a result of this decision; photographs indicate that most RNAS personnel were wearing 'landsmen's' kit by late 1914, although some men still appear in seamen's rig during 1915.

As we have seen, **Chief Petty Officers** did not wear seamen's kit, and it will be convenient to describe their **Class I** dress first to avoid repetition when describing Class III clothing. All of the following garments were produced in ultra dark blue fabric unless otherwise stated.

The CPO's cap had a blue crown, black mohair band and black leather peak and chin strap, the latter retained by black, fabric covered buttons. The badge was embroidered in metal wire on a black melton patch and consisted of a gold crown above a circular padded black velvet 'cushion' which was encircled by two strands of gold wire and bore a fouled anchor. In accordance with Military Branch practice the metal elements of the anchor were rendered in silver embroidery and the stock – the cross-bar at the top – and the rope in gold wire.

Air Mechanic 1st Class E.H. Basler in the issued single-breasted Class III blue serge uniform, with red eagle and propeller badge just visible on his right upper sleeve. (RAFM DB33)

ABOVE **Warrant Officer 2nd Grade H.J. Lloyd, RNAS. Warrant Officers wore the Officers' uniform and conformed to all the minor amendments to that dress in respect of cuff eagles and, as here, grey flannel trousers. (RAFM de Salis Album)**

ABOVE, RIGHT **Petty Officer E.G. Frost in double-breasted cloth jacket, gold wire rating badge and gilt Armoured Car branch collar badges. (RAFM DB19)**

The eight-button, double-breasted jacket was cut so as to be capable of fastening right up to the neck with a stand-and-fall collar; however, it was never worn in this manner, the upper part of the opening being folded down to form lapels and the collar turned over so as to resemble a roll-step collar. This adjustment would usually have had the effect of hiding the upper pair of buttons, but they were often so adjusted that they appeared in the cleft of the step below the collar. All buttons were of gilt metal and bore crowned fouled anchors. A pair of inset pockets with flaps was provided in the lower skirt, and two small buttons vertically at the rear of the cuff.

A single-breasted, six-button waistcoat was worn under the jacket with a white shirt and black tie. Wing or turn-down stiff collars are seen with two types of tie; the normal straight type, and a sort of false bow tie which fitted inside the V-aperture of the turn-down shirt collar. The waistcoat was cut so as not to show between the lapels of the jacket. Trousers and black laced ankle boots or shoes completed the outfit.

Although this is the uniform which is invariably seen in photographs, a Working Dress jacket existed which was of four-button, single-breasted form.

Two patterns of **Class III** jacket were ordered for wear by POs and Ratings. The first, for formal parade wear only, was exactly the same as that for CPOs but with black horn buttons instead of gilt ones. The second, for normal working wear, was a single-breasted, four-button garment with flapped, external, gussetted pockets and two small buttons at the rear of the cuff. These garments were worn with white shirt, black straight tie, a peaked cap bearing a red embroidered badge of exactly the same design as for CPOs, and either trousers or pantaloons and puttees with ankle boots.

* * *

It is clear that the management of dress in the Royal Navy was not conducted on the same lines as in the Army. In the Army men were issued with a free complete kit which was renewed periodically according to the calculated 'life' of the garments, the man's pay being regulated accordingly to take account of this 'free' issue. The Royal Navy made a genuinely free issue to a recruit, and thereafter the man was given an annual 'upkeep allowance', payable quarterly in advance, out of which the man could take up, on repayment, articles of kit as they became worn

out (Ad Monthly Order 414/1918). This allowance was considered part of the man's pay, and naval Ratings therefore owned their clothes whereas Army Other Ranks had theirs on loan from the state. In consequence Ratings exercised a great deal more freedom over how they modified and wore that part of their clothing which had been relegated to working dress.

As a war economy measure the issue of the double-breasted suit to air mechanics and aircraftmen was discontinued by AdWO 3501 of December 1916, and withdrawn from CPOs by AdWO 3884 of October 1917. The kit became optional, and photographic evidence indicates that it continued in use, many men providing it themselves, probably partially out of their own pockets and partially out of their uniform allowance. This explains the appearance of advertisements inserted in air station magazines by mens' outfitters and department stores, drawing attention to the availability of best suits at reasonable prices.

'Best suits' were made in 'cloth', by which was meant a smooth-textured, close-woven fabric often described as superfine or doeskin, while the working clothing was made in serge. More easily discernible from photographs is that badges of trade and rating were worn in red silk embroidery on serge and in gold thread on superfine cloth. (This did not, of course, apply to the cap badge, which was red for all rates below CPO.)

Flight Sub-Lieutenant Willie Davenport wearing the khaki Officers' Overseas Service Dress. Note the gilt breast eagle, bronze buttons, pale khaki cap cover, and almost invisible khaki-on-khaki cuff rank lace – a single stripe with the executive curl. (RAFM Box 144)

Men of No.8 Naval Squadron on the Somme, 1916. They all wear khaki, mostly General Service pattern, but the figure at right with cigarette wears the 1915 Economy Pattern jacket without pocket pleats and shoulder panels. He and the two men behind him also wear bronze cap badges. (RAFM PC1997/89/4)

1: Sergeant, Royal Flying Corps, 1913
2: Second Lieutenant, RFC; Full Dress, 1913-14
3: Leading Mechanic, Naval Wing, RFC; CFS Upavon, summer 1913

A

1: Lieutenant-Colonel, RFC; Mess Dress, 1913 Pattern
2: Flight Lieutenant, Royal Naval Air Service; Mess Dress, 1918
3: Lieutenant, Royal Flying Corps; Patrol Dress, 1917-18

1: Second Lieutenant, Observer, Royal Flying Corps, 1917-18
2: Captain, Staff Officer, Royal Flying Corps, 1916
3: Major, HLI/Royal Flying Corps, 1918

C

1: Petty Officer, RNAS Armoured Car unit; France, 1915
2: Flight Sub-Lieutenant, Observer, RNAS, August 1917
3: Flight Lieutenant, RNAS; France, 1916

D

1: Captain, Staff Officer, RFC; Palestine, late 1917
2: Flight Lieutenant, No.6 Wing, RNAS; Italy, December 1917
3: Flight Sergeant, RFC; India, 1917
4: Petty Officer, RNAS; East Africa, 1915

E

1: Airframe Rigger, No.8 Squadron, RNAS; Somme front, 1916
2: Leading Rating, RNAS; Dunkirk, autumn 1917
3: Petty Officer, No.2 Wing, RNAS; Salonika, 1916

F

1: Air Mechanic 1st Class, RFC; France, 1916-17
2: Captain, RFC; France or UK, 1918
3: Air Mechanic, RFC, 1912-1915

1: Official, Women's Auxiliary Army Corps, late 1917
2: Rating, Women's Royal Naval Service, early 1918
3: Member, Women's Auxiliary Army Corps, 1917
4: Deputy Divisional Director, WRNS, early 1918

It seems that towards the end of the war, and particularly after the formation of the Royal Air Force, the distinction between best suits and **working clothing** disappeared. Double-breasted jackets with gold badges were evidently worn for working wear, presumably because it was realised that, in due course, the wearing of RNAS uniform would cease and the RAF one would take over. As with the Officers, all non-commissioned ranks of the RNAS enclosed their caps in white covers between May and September.

The Ratings' khaki greatcoat worn with leather buttons, red-on-blue shoulder title, and red-on-khaki leading mechanic's badge – cf Plate E2. (RAFM Box 144)

Men who wore trousers instead of pantaloons and puttees were issued with a pair of brown cloth gaiters which fastened up the outside by means of three interconnecting cord loops threaded through a buckled strap at the top. The standard RN two-piece white overall suit was worn by those who transferred to the RNAS, but direct entrants were provided with two blue combination suits with a half-belt at the back and strapped ankles. These garments had visible metal buttons unlike the RFC overalls. Both CPOs and lower rates were permitted to wear blue and white small-checked shirts in working dress, though after December 1916 these were changed to grey flannel. Soft collars were permitted by AdWO 2818 of October 1916.

The **Rating's greatcoat** was a long, tubular, single-breasted garment with five large crowned fouled anchor black horn buttons and a wide fall collar. It had no shoulder straps and was cut very loose in the body, with a generous pleat from the shoulders to the hem. The fullness in the body, which this pleat allowed when required, was taken up in normal wear by a pair of long, plain-buttoned tabs at the rear waist. There was no rear central vent. A pair of flapped pockets with internal bags was provided in the skirt, and false circular cuffs were indicated by stitching.

RNAS Rating and Qualification Badges

Badges of rating, which indicated their wearer's competence as well as his relative rank, were worn on the left upper arm by all qualified ranks below CPOs. Chief Petty Officers did not wear them, as their uniform was visibly different from those of other ratings. The following badges were used:

Petty Officer Mechanic	Crossed fouled anchors in saltire with crown above
Leading Mechanic	Vertical fouled anchor
Air Mechanics 1st & 2nd Class	No badge

Immediately below these badges, Good Conduct badges appeared in the form of inverted chevrons of lace; the first was awarded for three years, the second for five more, and the third after a total of 13 years' service. The top line of the upper chevron was set 5ins below the shoulder seam.

Trade qualification badges, known as Branch badges, were worn by POs and Ratings on the right upper arm and by some CPOs on the collar. They consisted of a variety of symbols which related more to the trades of the old sailing navy than to the modern Dreadnought force. When applied to the new aerial service the symbolism was often very much at variance with the equipment or the function of the tradesman.

In addition, RNAS personnel usually wore their own branch of service device – an eagle with out-stretched wings – above the symbol. Special qualifications within the trade were designated by a star above the symbol; two stars, one above and one below, indicated that a man was specially qualified and was actually employed in duties at that level. The list below is compiled from surviving examples, documents and photographs.

Trade/Qualification	Device/s
Armament Mechanic*	Crossed axe and hammer in saltire overlaid with a horizontal gun barrel with a star above
Armament Instructor*	Crown and star above a horizontal gun barrel
Aerial Gun-Layer*	Star above a horizontal gun barrel
Airframe Mechanic (Carpenter)	Crossed axe and hammer
Air Mechanic (Engines)	Horizontal propeller
Airship Coxswain	Eight-spoke ship's wheel
Aeroplane Pilot	'Throttle' wheel with three internal spokes
Wireless Mechanic Telegraphist	Lightning flash between a pair of diving wings with a star above
Wireless Operator	W.T.
Motorboat Coxswain	Six-spoke ship's wheel
Motor Transport Driver	Vertical spoked motor vehicle wheel between two wings
Civil Branch	Large star
Physical Training Instructor	Crossed Indian clubs with a star above **

Notes:

* AdWO 3319, December 1916

** PTIs were introduced to the RNAS by AdWO 2776 of July 1917. The badge described above is taken from a contemporary illustrated pamphlet, but does not conform to the badges for either PTIs Class I or II in the RN, which had two stars above and below and one star above respectively, and were surmounted by crowns.

Air Mechanic 1st Class Edward Basler in Egypt, wearing Army KD with black horn crowned fouled anchor buttons, brown belt, pale khaki cap cover and Home Service pattern puttees. (RAFM PhDB 3)

All of these badges were produced on blue patches in red embroidery for wear on working serge, gold embroidery for the best suit; some examples exist in pale blue embroidery on white, for wear on Class II dress, the sailing rig. Chief Petty Officers did not have to wear trade badges and most did not do so. Ratings without trade qualifications wore the RNAS branch eagle only. Many examples were made up by tailors and there are consequently numerous variations in size and the details of the designs.

In addition certain other badges were produced for wear by special sections of the RNAS or the Reserve Forces of the Royal Navy acting in an air-related capacity. Ratings of the **Armoured Car** branch wore horizontal oval collar badges surmounted by an integral crown; they showed a Talbot armoured car facing to the left with 'R.N.A.S.' above and conjoined sprigs of laurel below. They were produced in gilding metal for wear on blue and in bronze for wear on khaki dress. These

The Officers of the Mesopotamia Seaplane Squadron with Squadron Commander Frederick Bowhill (later Air Chief Marshal), at Kut, 1915. 'Scruff order' prevails, though gold laced shoulder boards are worn, and one officer is using his Full Dress white Wolseley helmet with blue silk fold in the puggaree – right foreground. (RAFM Box 84)

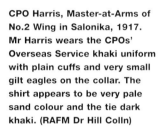

CPO Harris, Master-at-Arms of No.2 Wing in Salonika, 1917. Mr Harris wears the CPOs' Overseas Service khaki uniform with plain cuffs and very small gilt eagles on the collar. The shirt appears to be very pale sand colour and the tie dark khaki. (RAFM Dr Hill Colln)

Ratings' badges were definitely in use by early 1915 and are normally seen on blue clothing rather than khaki. Very rarely one sees Officers wearing gilt versions of this badge. Later, probably in 1917, Officers adopted pairs of armoured cars in profile, both pointing inwards, as collar badges. They exist in versions depicting the Talbot and the Lanchester armoured cars, the latter being used by No.1 Armoured Car Squadron in Russia.

A similar oval badge was produced in gilt metal for the **Armoured Train** service which operated in northern Belgium from September 1914 to April 1915. Within a border bearing NAVAL ARMOURED TRAINS was featured an armoured railway carriage overlaid by a winged Caduceus of Mercury, the wings extending horizontally beyond the top of the oval. The service was commanded by Commander Astle Scott Littlejohns, RN, who was specially attached to the RNAS for this duty. It is assumed that the operating personnel were also drawn from the RNAS.

On 3 September 1914 the Admiralty agreed to take over from the Army the anti-aircraft defence of London and other non-garrisoned towns until the manpower situation stabilised. The overall responsibility was placed with the Director of the Air Department. A 'special branch of the RNVR to be known as the **Anti-Aircraft Corps** of the Royal

CPO Robert Corner in East Africa, wearing working dress with his silver and gold CPO's badge on his Wolseley helmet. (RAFM B.Cook Album)

Naval Air Service' was formed round a cadre drawn from the Metropolitan Police. As the force expanded Ratings of the RNAS, mostly drivers and mechanics, were posted to it for duty. Petty Officers and men of the original London force wore embroidered red badges on the collar only with the initials 'RNVR' above 'AAC', sometimes embroidered in straight lines, sometimes with the upper line slightly curved. CPOs wore the same lettering arranged so as to encircle a crown, but in gold embroidery. By spring 1915 the Corps had become fully integrated into the RNAS, and on 21 April badges incorporating the letters 'RNAS' were approved to replace the RNVR badges.

All ranks were authorised to wear **wound stripes** on the left cuff, half an inch above the eagle for Officers, made up of a 2-in length of gold Russia braid positioned vertically (AdWO 2176 September 1916).

RNAS Leather Firearms Equipment

As the Royal Navy had often provided sailors to act as soldiers in the campaigns of the 19th century it had developed suitable ammunition-carrying equipment for riflemen. The pattern in use in 1914 was known as Accoutrements for Seamen Pattern 1901. The set was made in brown leather with brass fittings, and comprised a 1¾ in wide waistbelt with plain pin buckle, two rectangular pouches, a bayonet or cutlass frog, a mess tin with brown canvas carrier, and braces. A separate brown canvas haversack, a waterbottle and a bandolier were also provided. The pouches, frog and mess tin carrier slid onto the belt by means of leather loops and were supported by braces, passing through metal rings on the top of the pouches and hooking back on themselves. At the rear, the braces hooked into holes along the centre line of the belt on either side of the centrally-positioned mess tin. Additional short straps and a brass ring connected the top of the carrier to the braces just below the point where they crossed. The haversack was worn from right shoulder to left hip under the equipment, and the bandolier and waterbottle from left shoulder to right hip over it. The pouches carried 60 rounds of 0.303in ammunition each, and the bandolier 60 rounds, in clips of five, in 12 flapped pockets arranged along its entire length. It fastened with a double-pin buckle at the shoulder, and a steadying strap secured it to the waistbelt at the lowest point.

Officers and CPOs armed with automatic pistols or revolvers used the same belt, braces and mess tin carrier, but replaced the right pouch with the holster and the left one with a smaller pouch. The flap of the revolver pouch bore six external loops for ready-use rounds, plus 48 rounds inside; the pistol pouch carried two ready-loaded magazines and 77 rounds.

RNAS Overseas Service Dress – Officers

Soon after the war began RNAS units equipped with both aircraft and armoured cars started operating in Flanders, based on Dunkirk. It is clear that all personnel continued to wear blue clothing during 1914, but by the spring of 1915 Officers had acquired distinctive khaki uniforms. The standard Home Service cap was worn with a pale khaki cover over the blue crown. The jacket was a conventional single-breasted type with shoulder straps, four flap-and-button pockets and a central rear vent. Buttons were of the RNAS design in bronze, and rank was indicated on the cuffs in khaki lace with a woven texture to make it more visible. Small clothes, Sam Browne and brown footwear were as for Army uniform, though trousers appeared with turn-ups. On this jacket Officers engaged in flying duties wore only one gilt eagle above the left breast pocket. The uniform was authorised by AdWO 2842 of November 1916, but this was obviously an order making formal a practice already well established. This dress remained in use until the end of the war and underwent no significant changes.

Some Officers provided themselves with caps with khaki fabric peaks and crowns made up in the same cloth as the jacket, i.e. not within a cover; there is some indication of brown leather chin straps as well. Photographs also indicate that Army style rank pips were sometimes worn on the shoulder straps, but it is unclear when this practice was introduced or whether it had official sanction. Bronze eagles also appear to have been used instead of gilt ones. A version of the watch coat in khaki fabric was authorised for wear with this kit.

RNAS Overseas Service Dress – Ratings

Though Officers went into khaki before Ratings did, their men were not far behind. During 1915 the relatively small numbers of men serving in the eastern Mediterranean were supplied with General Service pattern clothing which they wore in a style entirely their own. The second batch of recipients belonged to the units sent to support the RFC in preparation for the Battle of the Somme in late spring 1916. Photographs of No.8 Squadron RNAS clearly show these men in double-breasted, Mounted Services-type-greatcoats, some of which bear crescent-shaped (i.e. downward-curving) shoulder titles with 'R.N.A.S.' embroidered in red on dark blue (see Plate F1). Although most men were clothed in 1908 GS pattern jackets it is evident that some were issued with the new 'war economy' pattern of 1915. This variant was the same shape, but had no pleats in the breast pockets and no rubbing panels on the front of the shoulders. Both patterns appear in photographs with shoulder titles. Chief Petty Officers wore a khaki version of their single-breasted clothing with khaki shirt and tie. Rating and qualification badges on this clothing almost always show up as the red-on-blue variety, though red-on-khaki versions as used by the Royal Naval Division can certainly be discerned from 1917 onwards. CPOs sometimes wore small gold metal eagles on the collar.

RNAS Tropical Uniform – Officers

Service in Italy, East Africa, Aden, Mesopotamia and in the Aegean during the summer months

Air Mechanic Percy Mercer on leave in Bombay, 1917. He evidently had a bazaar tailor make him up a suit of cotton clothing cut in almost exactly the same style as his blue Home Service suit. The fabric is thicker than issued KD, however, and a pale mid-brown rather than sand colour. (RAFM PC1995/176/1)

gave rise to the need for Khaki Drill clothing, which was not normal wear for naval personnel, whose tropical clothing was white. The jacket was very similar to that worn by Army Officers, being single-breasted with four bronze rope and crowned eagle buttons and with flapped, buttoned breast and skirt pockets, the upper pair pleated, the lower gussetted. Shoulder straps were provided to secure the Sam Browne brace, and rank appeared in pale khaki lace in normal naval fashion on the cuffs. It was usually worn with trousers but could appear with breeches, puttees and brown ankle boots or field boots. Headgear consisted of the standard cap with khaki or white cover, or a Wolseley helmet. The Dress Regulations state that the helmet was to be the standard white Full Dress tropical helmet worn with a white puggaree whose top fold was made in dark blue silk; a KD-covered helmet might, however, be worn when Officers were '...exposed to enemy fire'. Shirt and tie were of pale khaki.

This, at least, is what the uniform should have been; but almost all activities seem to have been undertaken in working dress, and it is extremely rare to find photographs of RNAS Officers in hot climates dressed in full uniform. Comfort was obviously the prime consideration, and the universal garb seems to have been reduced to shorts, open-necked shirts with rolled sleeves, and long stockings with shoes.

RNAS Tropical Uniform – Ratings

The same motley appearance is to be found amongst non-commissioned RNAS personnel who adapted their kit to the extremely harsh climates in which they worked. It is clear that all were issued with tropical uniform, but, as with their Officers, this seems to have been worn very rarely, probably only for the most formal parades and when on leave in Cairo or elsewhere. Other Ranks' KD kit of Army pattern was used in its various forms, the metal buttons sometimes being replaced by black horn. Personnel serving in Aden who had access to bazaar tailors sometimes had suits made up on similar lines to their single-breasted blue clothing for wear with collar and tie. The Wolseley helmet appears to have been universally issued, though caps with or without covers are also seen. It appears that no KD badges were available officially, and very few seem to have been made locally. CPOs wore single-breasted suits cut for wear with a sand-coloured collar and tie, with gilt buttons and false pointed cuffs.

RNAS Mess Dress

Officers continued to use Mess Dress in the UK throughout the war. It comprised a short double-breasted jacket with three buttons on each side and a double button and link to fasten it. Lapels, which were not faced in silk, were cut with a cleft and provided with four pairs of buttonholes, as if the jacket was supposed to fasten up to the neck. Two slit pockets appeared in the lower front sides, and rank – with eagles, observer badges and stars as appropriate – on the cuffs in gold. The waistcoat was cut low and round and was fitted with lapels and four buttons. Plain trousers were worn with Wellington boots. Shirts were stiff-fronted with wing collars, gold studs and black bow ties.

RNAS Working Dress

A two-piece, single-breasted white overall suit was used by all naval Ratings, but when the RNAS was formed a blue combination suit was

Member Dora Ramsay has already transferred to the WRAF; though she still wears the khaki WAAC motorcyclist's tunic, she has removed the shoulder straps – which would have borne a maroon centre stripe. Her cap badge is the red RAF type, but she still sports RFC shoulder titles. (RAFM 1998/44/1)

introduced for air mechanics. It was similar to the first such garment used by the RFC, having a half-belt at the rear and ankle straps, but its buttons were visible. Pale blue on white badges were certainly worn on the white suit but, it seems, none were worn on the blue. Black oilskins were also available as foul weather gear.

THE WOMEN'S SERVICES

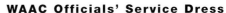

From as early as 1915 it became apparent that Great Britain was engaged in a prolonged war which would require the mobilisation of every national resource. The Women's Services started as unofficial, voluntary bodies which provided largely domestic assistance to the Armed Forces; female medical staff already had a long and distinguished history within the Army. Gradually gaining acceptance from the military authorities, by March 1917 the Women's Auxiliary Army Corps was formed on the foundations laid by Lady Londonderry's Women's Legion. Naturally some of the personnel were attached to the RFC. Similarly, the Admiralty had been approached with the offer of female assistance to the Royal Navy, and in November the Women's Royal Naval Service was formed, some of its young ladies being attached for duty to the RNAS.

WOMEN'S AUXILIARY ARMY CORPS

The Corps was not permitted military ranks but used Grade titles; its Officers were known as 'officials' and its Other Ranks were referred to as 'members'; supervisory staff – the equivalents of NCOs – were collectively called 'subordinate officials'. Titles are given in the table below.

WAAC Officials' Service Dress

The Service Dress devised for WAAC 'Officers' was khaki throughout. Headdress consisted of a fabric peaked cap with a large, soft crown gathered into a band, a brown leather chin strap and a bronze badge bearing 'W' over 'AA' over 'C' within a wreath. This was replaced by a khaki domed felt hat with a broad brim and brown band bearing the Corps badge; though neater, smaller caps with a turned-up rear peak were also used. The jacket was single-breasted, usually with three buttons, shoulder straps and flap-and-button lower pockets. A roll step collar was decorated above the step with the same badges as worn on the cap, though smaller versions were produced later. A cloth belt fastened with two buttons about 6ins apart at the front, and a round-ended tab about the same length with two buttons positioned in the centre rear of the belt – this feature was non-functional. Two small uniform buttons appeared, vertically, at the rear of the cuffs. The back of the jacket was plain with no pleat or vents. Buttons were usually of leather though gilding metal

Chief Controller Helen Gwynne-Vaughan (left) with other WAAC officials, London 1918. The chief controller sports a voluminous cap with a turned-up rear peak. Note large size collar badges, gaiters and mourning band. (J. & A. Poucher Collection)

General Service pattern examples were sometimes used.

The shoulder straps were decorated with a stripe of colour, denoting the wearer's function, running up the centre: sky blue for Controllers, orange for Administrators, green for Recruiting Controllers, purple for General Duties Officials. Officials acting with the Provost's Branch seem to have used black with narrow orange edges, but it seems unlikely that the colours denoting more specific and menial jobs were worn by officials. On the shoulder straps grades were shown by bronze badges, either fleur-de-lys or roses or a combination of both according to the following table:

WRNS Officers at Torquay Air Station, November 1918. Although assistant principals were not originally ordered to wear the diamond above their rank lace it was adopted during 1918. The lace and hat badge embroidery is a rich mid-blue colour, though the film emulsion shows it as pale as their gilt buttons. Note handkerchiefs in pockets, and brown gloves. (RAFM AC1998/68/3)

WAAC Officials' Grades:

Grade	Stationed/ responsibilities	Fleur-de-lys	Rose
Controller-in-Chief	UK	–	3
Chief Controller	France	1	2 conjoined
Deputy Chief Controller	UK	1	2
Deputy Chief Controller	France	1	1
Section Controller	UK	1	1
Asst. Section Controller	UK	2	–
Area Controller	at HQs of Commands, some areas & base ports in France	1	–
Clothing Controller	UK	–	3
Technical Assistant Controller	Inspector of Women's Work	–	1
Unit Administrator	Large hostel	–	3
Deputy Administrator	Small hostel	–	2
Deputy Administrator	Asst., large hostel	–	1
Assistant Administrator	–	–	1
Quartermistress Class I	Large hostel	–	2
Quartermistress Class II	–	–	1

A plain skirt hanging 12ins above the ground was worn with khaki shirt and tie and brown stockings and shoes. Officials wore double-breasted fleece cloth greatcoats with shoulder straps with coloured inserts and grade badges, large collars (often trimmed in fur), with a buttoned belt and bronze or leather buttons. The shade of officials' uniforms varied from standard greenish khaki to yellowish-brown. Cap badges were often backed with a piece of fabric in function colour.

WAAC Members' Clothing

All grades of members wore a slightly greyish-khaki coatfrock – a rather shapeless single-breasted, six-button garment falling to 12ins above the ground. It had a button belt with its distinctive tab at the rear, buttoned cuffs with an opening in the front of the sleeve, shoulder straps, and a plain detachable collar in brown for workers and white for subordinate officials (NCO equivalents). Shoulder straps bore coloured centre stripes indicative of the members' function: clerks, brown; domestic workers, red; drivers, claret/maroon; general duties, purple. In addition a title, 'WAAC' embroidered in pale buff on khaki, was sewn on the outer end of the shoulder strap. Buttons were made of leather or composition – some stamped with the Royal Arms, some quite plain – worn as a consequence of AO200 of July 1917 which ordered them for all Army ranks due to the metal shortage. Subordinate officials wore appointment badges on the right upper sleeve: a brown rose within a brown and pale buff wreath embroidered on a small horizontal oval khaki patch for 'forewomen' (sergeant equivalents); and a wreath alone for 'assistant forewomen' (corporal equivalents).

These WAACs were serving with the RFC before 1 April 1918. They have replaced their brass WAAC hat badge with the RAF embroidered type, but otherwise their uniform is unchanged. Their coatfrocks still have standard RFC shoulder-titles and some shoulder straps retain the 'duties' colour. Note the different shape of khaki hats. (RAFM PC 1998/164/24)

A brown, domed, broad-brimmed felt hat, later changed to khaki, with brown band and gilding metal badge, khaki stockings and black shoes completed the outfit. The serge greatcoat was a long single-breasted, six-button garment with a large collar, plain shoulder straps, a buttoned belt, false cuffs, and two flapped pockets angled or horizontal – in the front of the skirts. The WAAC embroidered title appeared across the outer end of the shoulder straps. Subordinate officials wore their appointment badges on the right sleeve of their greatcoats. Members were also permitted to provide themselves with waterproof coats of civilian pattern and all were issued with gaiters for foul weather wear.

No jewellery or other decorations were officially permitted to be worn by WAACs apart from wedding rings, but photographs indicate that this restriction was frequently ignored. 'Sweetheart brooches', often featuring the RFC wings, appear quite commonly, and former members of the Women's Legion were allowed to wear their original cap badge as a brooch on the coatfrock and the lapel of the greatcoat.

One of the roles to which women took enthusiastically was as drivers and motorcycle messengers. For these duties the long coatfrock was inconvenient, and the garment was produced as a mid-thigh length tunic and issued with a skirt.

Wren in the cap, jacket and skirt uniform worn by MT drivers. The driving gauntlets were evidently a private purchase.

Motorcycle riders often, but not always, wore breeches. They all wore laced boots of various lengths. Many drivers retained the cap rather than the felt hat and motorcyclists certainly did so. All were entitled to motoring goggles and gauntlets, many choosing to provide themselves with fur-backed examples.

Many members of the Women's Legion Motor Drivers Section worked for the RFC before the creation of the WAAC, and adopted the Corps' shoulder title on their own dress. Women's Legion dress was a jacket and skirt cut very similar to those later worn by WAAC officials, the principal difference being that the lapels of the Legion jacket were longer and the shirt thereby more visible. As many women retained their WL clothing and wore it with WAAC and RFC badges, it is often difficult to identify which organisation the wearer actually belonged to at the time the photograph was taken or what 'rank' she held. It is clear, however, that officials never rode motorcycles as part of their duties and probably only rarely drove themselves in cars.

The WAACs attached to the RFC were engaged in domestic, clerical or technical duties. They obviously quickly identified with the Corps, and all grades adopted the standard 'Royal Flying Corps' embroidered shoulder title for their jackets or coatfrocks. Photographic evidence indicates that shoulder straps were often removed from the coatfrock and that broad, dark-coloured ties, either dark brown or black, were worn by members. These additions often brought with them tie pins or small brooches.

WOMEN'S ROYAL NAVAL SERVICE

Like the War Office, the Admiralty eventually had to concede that female labour was necessary to the war effort, and the WRNS was set up in November 1917.

WRNS Officers' Service Dress

Officers wore the standard RN 'monkey jacket' tailored to the female figure with five gilt buttons on each side, four being visible. A white shirt and black tie accompanied a plain four-panel skirt, slightly gathered at the rear, falling to 9ins from the ground. Shoes and stockings were black. Headdress was a black velour tricorne hat with flat crown, black mohair band and brim edging, finished at the front with a badge. This was a version of the standard RN cap badge but with the silver anchor and 'WRNS' in gold wire on a padded round patch and the laurel leaves embroidered in a bright mid-blue silk. The same colour was used for rank braid in broad (1⅜in), medium (½in) or narrow (¼in) width, which appeared on the cuffs according to the following table. Instead of the 'executive curl' senior ranks wore a hollow diamond of half-inch lace measuring 1½ins along each outer face.

Rank	Broad	Medium	Narrow	Diamond (Y/N)
Director	1	1	–	Y
Deputy Director	1	–	–	Y
Assistant Director	–	4	–	Y
Deputy Assistant Director	–	3	–	Y
Divisional Director	–	2	1*	Y
Deputy Divisional Director	–	2	–	Y
Principal	–	3	–	N
Deputy Principal	–	2	–	N
Assistant Principal	–	1	–	N
Quarters Supervisor	–	1	–	**

Notes:

* between the two medium laces
** above three buttons on the cuff

The blue embroidery and lace faded to a pale petrol-blue colour which stood out clearly against the almost black uniform. The two senior ranks wore buttons which had the fouled anchor enclosed within a laurel wreath. Those ranks which were not originally ordered to wear the diamond above their rank lace acquired it during 1918, probably as a result of AdWO 3224 of October 1918.

WRNS and WRAFs at Warsash Air Station, 1918. The former, mostly clerical staff – note crossed quills sleeve badge – are in the standard coatfrock, while their CPO (front right) wears the more elegant jacket and skirt, with scallop shell badges for Domestic staff on the collar. The Officer (rear right) still wears WRNS uniform but has changed her hat badge on joining the WRAF. (RAFM Album 243)

WRNS Ratings' Service Dress

Like the WAAC, WRNS Ratings wore a coatfrock. It was made of very dark blue rough serge with four plain black buttons, a single-button belt and flapped, buttoned pockets. Cuffs buttoned at the front. Originally it was fitted with a small blue jean sailor's collar without the characteristic white lacing; this deficiency was soon made good, however. The blue hat was a plain round affair with the crown gathered into a brim, the back of which was often turned up. It carried a black silk cap tally embroidered with a gold crowned fouled anchor between 'W.R.' and 'N.S.'; white covers were approved for WRNS Ratings in July 1918. Black stockings and laced shoes completed the outfit. Rating badges were worn exactly as for the RN, and category badges were worn on the right in the following designs, both being embroidered in bright mid-blue on dark blue patches:

Domestic Worker	Scallop shell
Clerical Staff	Crossed quill pens
Motor Transport Drivers	Three-spoked wheel
Store-keepers, Porters & Messengers	Crossed keys
Postwomen & Telegraphists	Envelope
Signals Staff	Vertical arrow with horizontal thunderbolt
Technical Staff	Crossed hammers
General Duties	Star

Chief Petty Officers wore a double-breasted jacket with six gilt buttons and two on each cuff. Their category badges appeared in small size on the collar in blue silk, not gold thread. They wore the same hat as Ratings, but with a black mohair band and a cap badge of blue silk with a gold wire fouled anchor. A blue skirt and white shirt with black tie completed the set.

Motor transport drivers wore similar clothing but with black horn buttons on the jacket. Their headgear was a stylish blue cap with tally. Goggles and fur-backed gauntlets were also worn. The working dress of other Ratings varied considerably. A coatfrock overall in a palish mid-blue was worn with the sailor collar, as well as a plain oatmeal-coloured 'duster cloth' overall gown with its own collar. Duster cloth combination suits and jacket and trouser suits also appear in photographs.

BIBLIOGRAPHY

Dress Regulations for Officers of the Army 1911
King's Regulations 1912
Army Orders 1912-1918
Record of Sealed Patterns of Army Clothing (National Army Museum microfilm)
Service with the Army, Helen Gwynne-Vaughan, Hutchinson, London ND
Admiralty Weekly Orders, PRO Adm 182/4-13
WRNS Clothing 1917, PRO Adm 116/3455
Dress Regulations contained in *The Navy Lists* 1914-1918
Clothing Regulations for CPOs, Seamen and Boys of the Royal Navy, 1913
The Anti-Aircraft Corps, PRO Adm 116/1344

OPPOSITE **Detail from a group photograph of Major William D.S. Sanday, DSO, MC, and Officers of No.19 Squadron RFC, 1917, displaying a typical mixture of uniform types which were common across all units. Field Service caps – an exclusively RFC headgear – are being worn with regimental uniforms and RFC cap badges with regimental collar badges. Several men in the original group wear flying boots (e.g. front left). (RAFM DB 88)**

THE PLATES

A1: Sergeant Pilot, Royal Flying Corps, 1913

This is the second version of the Other Ranks' 1912 Pattern jacket. The form of the garment has been improved by extending the flap over to the shoulder, but the pockets are still the inconvenient vertical type, and there are no shoulder straps. Until May 1914 sergeants wore only the three-chevron badge of rank without the distinctive propeller.

A2: Second Lieutenant, Royal Flying Corps, Full Dress, 1913-14

The extremely rare Officers' Full Dress of the RFC illustrated from an example in the RAF Museum collection. Only direct entrants to the Corps would have had to provide themselves with it, and it can have been worn on few occasions. No photograph of it in use is known to the author. The Dress Regulations make no mention of the carriage of swords, though it is inconceivable that they were not worn; the infantry Officers' 1897 Pattern weapon was certainly worn by the RFC with Service Dress and it has been speculatively added here, on gold slings with a dark blue centre stripe slung from the 'web' belt worn beneath the girdle, as mentioned in the 1911 Dress Regulations and King's Regulations 1912.

A3: Leading Mechanic, Naval Wing, Royal Flying Corps; CFS Upavon, summer 1913

Photographs indicate that Royal Navy personnel wore their Class II seamen's clothing in both the dark blue serge version and the white cotton 'hot climates' version while serving at the Central Flying School. Strictly speaking the latter should not have been worn in England, and it was certainly not well adapted to the castor oil, grease and exhaust grime of the early aero engines. By 1915 all RNAS personnel had been re-kitted with Class III dress of dark blue jacket, pantaloons and peaked cap.

B1: Lieutenant-Colonel, Royal Flying Corps, Mess Dress, 1913 Pattern

Mess Dress for RFC Officers was described in Army Order 378 of 1913. This illustration is based on the only known set, made according to the pattern for LtCol Frederick Llewelyn Scholto for wear at a reunion in 1928.

B2: Flight Lieutenant, Royal Naval Air Service, Mess Dress, 1918

Unlike the Army, the Royal Navy continued to wear Mess Dress throughout the war. The example in this plate belonged to Flight Lieutenant William Jerome de Salis, DSC (note the miniature worn with this order of dress), who served as an Acting Flight Commander in 1918 and thus wore the star badge of this appointment above his rank lace.

B3: Lieutenant, Royal Flying Corps, Patrol Dress, 1917-18

Patrol Dress was approved for wear throughout the Army and appears commonly in the pre-war photographs of the Central Flying School. This illustration is based on the uniform made for Lieutenant Norman Pellew by Rogers & Co. of Covent Garden in September 1917. This form of dress would not have been worn outside the United Kingdom.

C1: Second Lieutenant, Observer, Royal Flying Corps, 1917-18

He wears the 1917 Pattern jacket with rank on the shoulder straps. Some jackets of this type were produced without the false pointed cuff. Breeches tended to be khaki or slightly varied shades of beige – grey-buff. Stockings and shoes were typically worn as working dress. The 'Gor' Blimey' cap had little stiffening in the crown and had a neck flap with a supplementary fabric chin strap which could be let down in foul weather to create a sort of balaclava helmet. The RFC dog jacket (from the RAF Museum's collection) was made for an officer's pet by the squadron tailor. It has flying badges on both shoulders, the observer's on the left and the pilot's on the right.

C2: Captain, Staff Officer, Royal Flying Corps, 1916

This Officer wears the 1915 Pattern jacket with rank shown by pips on the laced cuff patch. His cap is of the early type with wire stiffener. He wears the second version of the RFC Staff Officers' armband, introduced in February 1916. This general style of uniform remained in use throughout the war. The khaki colour of Officers' jackets varied considerably in shade, and their shirts and ties could range from dark, rich green-khaki through pale olive to brownish-yellow. Ties also varied in fabric, some being smooth, others knitted.

C3: Major, Royal Flying Corps, 1918

The continued wear of their former regimental dress by individual Officers resulted in some very varied 'RFC' uniforms. This portrait of Major Alexander Paul Davidson in early 1918 shows him in Highland Light Infantry uniform, with the pilot's badge as the only indication that he was serving with the RFC. As an Officer of field rank he wears riding breeches, in his regiment's Mackenzie tartan, and the dark blue puttees of pre-war days which were still permitted with this kit. Major Davidson served at HQ Northern Command, York. Photographs and watercolours exist of kilted Highland Officers in the RFC, but it appears that such colourful dress was not used in France. Most Officers who continued to wear their original regimental or corps uniforms were only distinguishable by their RFC cap and collar badges.

D1: Petty Officer of an RNAS Armoured Car unit; France, 1915

He wears the single-breasted Class III blue serge uniform with canvas gaiters and the 1901 Pattern 'Equipment for Seamen', here configured with the revolver and its special ammunition pouch with loops for ready-use rounds. His two chevrons indicate eight years' unblemished service.

D2: Flight Sub-Lieutenant, Observer, RNAS, August 1917

White cap covers were worn during the summer months, and grey flannels were permitted in working dress in hot weather. From late June 1917 observers were ordered to wear

D3: Flight Lieutenant, Royal Naval Air Service; France, 1916

From 1915 Officers serving in units on the French coast were ordered to wear khaki clothing instead of dark blue. The uniform was similar to the Army Service Dress but with naval rank shown in khaki braid. The eagle badge moved from the cuff to the left breast. Brown footwear was ordered for this uniform. It was permitted to have caps made up in khaki fabric, sometimes including a fabric peak, and to wear them with bronze metal cap badges 'when under enemy fire'.

E1: Captain, Staff Officer, Royal Flying Corps; Palestine, late 1917

The date of this figure is set by his staff tabs in French grey with crimson gimp, introduced in August 1917, but the rest of his kit was common for the whole war period. He has chosen to wear light-weight fabric gaiters instead of leather ones or warm woollen puttees. Rank insignia is in bronze, though his buttons are gilt.

E2: Flight Lieutenant W.J. de Salis, No.6 Wing, RNAS; Otranto, Italy, December 1917

The RNAS tropical dress was identical in cut to the RNAS khaki Service Dress. De Salis was awarded his Distinguished Service Cross for operations with the Home Fleet in the North Sea. Now serving in south-east Italy, he sports the white naval version of the Wolseley helmet with its dark blue puggaree fold. Some helmets were made up in KD fabric, but still with the blue puggaree fold. It appears that flight and squadron commanders' stars were not produced for wear on KD clothing.

E3: Flight Sergeant, Royal Flying Corps; Risalpur, India, 1917

Pith hats were an alternative to the Wolseley helmet for wear in the tropics; they were flatter in the crown, and the brim curled under all round. Some RFC personnel in India adopted a silk puggaree flash in the Corps colours of dark blue, light blue and red, which is not seen in Palestine or Egypt. The 1908 Pattern KD frock had small buttons throughout and badges attached by hooks so as to be removable for washing. A brass shoulder title, indistinguishable from that worn on Full Dress, was also used in India in preference to the embroidered title.

E4: Petty Officer, Royal Naval Air Service; East Africa, 1915

Petty Officer Thomas Alexander McKim served in German East Africa with the RNAS from April 1915. A photograph of him shows this typical working clothing, and the application of loops to the underside of his large sleeve rating badge so that it could be slid onto the shirt shoulder strap. It was a common practice for Ratings to wear their cap badges on the front of the puggaree of their Wolseley helmets.

All RFC overalls were identical in cut. This mechanic wears the one-piece khaki cotton drill combination of 1917; cf the earlier blue type worn in Plate G3. (RAFM Box 97)

F1: Airframe Rigger, No.8 Squadron, RNAS; The Somme, 1916

RNAS personnel serving in France were kitted out with Army clothing – sometimes, as here, the 'war economy' jacket, worn with blue and red badges and this unusual downward-curving shoulder title. His blue cap is encased in a khaki cover and bears a bronze metal Ratings' cap badge.

F2: Leading Rating, RNAS; Dunkirk, autumn 1917

Taken directly from a photograph – it is surprising to see a white cap cover instead of a khaki one. The RNAS serving in Europe adopted a short khaki greatcoat on which Ratings wore red-on-blue and red-on-khaki badges.

F3: Petty Officer, No.2 Wing, RNAS; Salonika, 1916

Taken from a photograph, this figure wears the jacket of his two-piece overall working suit, with khaki breeches and puttees but the waistcoat from his Home Service Class III dress. As naval personnel owned their own clothes and were responsible for their replacement, they could acquire a stock to wear out as working clothing.

G1: Air Mechanic 1st Class, RFC; France, 1916-17

The 1914 Pattern greatcoat with shoulder straps could be worn either with the full shoulder title or the 'R.F.C.' initial type. His appointment badge is worn on the right sleeve only. The cut of the Officers' coat was the same, though they tended to use the 'British Warm' style coat after 1914.

G2: Captain, RFC; France or UK, 1918

The 1914 Pattern 'maternity' jacket was often worn with trousers in working dress or when off duty. Walking sticks with handles or canes with knobs came in all styles, and were sometimes made from timber salvaged from crashed aircraft. This Officer wears the ribbon of the 1914 Star, issued during 1917. The service chevrons on his right forearm each indicate one year with an operational unit, the red chevron for 1914 and the blue for subsequent years.

G3: Air Mechanic, Royal Flying Corps, 1912-1915

The blue overall worn by this engine fitter remained in use into 1915 and would have been worn concurrently with the new brown pattern until worn out. All overalls appear to have been of the same cut. Rank badges were not worn.

H1: Official, Women's Auxiliary Army Corps, late 1917

She wears the standard officials' uniform with the orange inserts of administration personnel on her shoulder straps, and bronze badges. The fabric and shade of WAAC uniforms varied considerably and so did the button arrangement; this is accounted for by tailors' variations and the conversion of some Women's Legion clothing. Like the latter organisation, some officials placed fabric patches of their duties colour behind the 'W/AA/C' hat badge.

H2: Rating, Women's Royal Naval Service, early 1918

Though certainly more prickly to wear, the thick serge WRNS coatfrock was a warmer garment than its WAAC equivalent.

Wren of the Clerical branch. Note the unevenly spaced buttons, the coarse serge material, the difference in fabric between the coatfrock and the hat and jean collar, and the 'W.R./anchor/N.S.' tally. The hat is secured by two pins. (J. & A. Poucher Collection)

The neckline varies on almost all examples, either due to modification by the women or contractors' variations. The blue jean collar was originally issued without white braiding, but this was soon added. This figure shows the Technical branch category badge of crossed hammers.

H3: Member, Women's Auxiliary Army Corps, 1917

The War Office was distinctly ungenerous in the clothing it issued to WAAC 'Other Ranks'; the coatfrock was thin and the quality of some of the garments left much to be desired. The dyes used in the original brown hats were defective and they assumed a pinkish tinge when they faded. Members who had previously served with the Women's Legion were permitted to wear their old hat badges as a brooch on their WAAC uniform. Many appear to have polished them so much that the bronze finish disappeared and they became bright yellow metal. Note the double shoulder titles, 'WAAC' on the end of the straps and 'ROYAL FLYING/CORPS' at the top of the sleeve.

H4: Deputy Divisional Director, Women's Royal Naval Service, early 1918

WRNS Officers' uniform conformed very closely to that of their male colleagues, unlike that worn by the WAAC. Surviving examples show that the blue dye used for their hat badges and rank lace was particularly unstable, and even on photographs of the period these distinctions show up as much brighter than one would expect – they faded to a vivid 'petrol' blue.

The Corporals' Mess, Risalpur, India, 14 May 1917. A couple of members wear the four-pocket version of the KD jacket, while most wear the two-pocket variant with curved gilding metal 'R.F.C.' titles on the shoulder straps, and small buttons. Note the pith hat in the foreground, with the RFC silk flash on the left side. (RAFM Box 150)

COMPANION SERIES FROM OSPREY

CAMPAIGN
Concise, authoritative accounts of history's decisive military encounters. Each 96-page book contains over 90 illustrations including maps, orders of battle, colour plates, and three-dimensional battle maps.

WARRIOR
Definitive analysis of the appearance, weapons, equipment, tactics, character and conditions of service of the individual fighting man throughout history. Each 64-page book includes full-colour uniform studies in close detail, and sectional artwork of the soldier's equipment.

NEW VANGUARD
Comprehensive histories of the design, development and operational use of the world's armoured vehicles and artillery. Each 48-page book contains eight pages of full-colour artwork including a detailed cutaway.

ORDER OF BATTLE
The most detailed information ever published on the units which fought history's great battles. Each 96-page book contains comprehensive organisation diagrams supported by ultra-detailed colour maps. Each title also includes a large fold-out base map.

ELITE
Detailed information on the organisation, appearance and fighting record of the world's most famous military bodies. This series of 64-page books, each containing some 50 photographs and diagrams and 12 full-colour plates, will broaden in scope to cover personalities, significant military techniques, and other aspects of the history of warfare which demand a comprehensive illustrated treatment.

AIRCRAFT OF THE ACES
Focuses exclusively on the elite pilots of major air campaigns, and includes unique interviews with surviving aces sourced specifically for each volume. Each 96-page volume contains up to 40 specially commissioned artworks, unit listings, new scale plans and the best archival photography available.

COMBAT AIRCRAFT
Technical information from the world's leading aviation writers on the century's most significant military aircraft. Each 96-page volume contains up to 40 specially commissioned artworks, unit listings, new scale plans and the best archival photography available.